PORTRAIT OF AN INDUSTRY

PORTRAIT OF AN INDUSTRY

THE AMBERLEY ARCHIVE

AMBERLEY

First published 2014

Amberley Publishing
The Hill, Stroud, Gloucestershire, GL5 4EP
www.amberley-books.com

Copyright © The Amberley Archive

The right of the Amberley Archive to be identified as the Authors of this work has been
asserted in accordance with the Copyrights, Designs and Patents Act 1988.

ISBN 978 1 4456 4258 1 (print)
ISBN 978 1 4456 4268 0 (ebook)

British Library Cataloguing in Publication Data.
A catalogue record for this book is available from the British Library.

Typesetting by Amberley Publishing.
Printed in Great Britain.

CONTENTS

INTRODUCTION

Many books have been written about the GWR. It goes without saying that many of these will deal with the history of the GWR and its subsidiaries in far more depth and detail than this one. However, this title will hopefully take a slightly different look at the railway giant of the twentieth century. As the title suggests, we hope to focus on the company's effect on the industries it involved itself in – not only transport itself, but the various methods it used to evolve and grow throughout the 1900s.

One key feature we will cover is advertising, as throughout its life the company exploited many media, both old and new, in order to promote not only its services but also the locations they served, thereby expanding an industry that today is its own powerhouse – tourism.

Another area we will look at in some detail is how innovation and standardisation produced specific features and engineering marvels which survive today. We will look at the station buildings, bridges, tunnels and other constructs created by Brunel, his contemporaries and successors in the service of the GWR, and how they changed the very landscape of the country.

And finally, as no book about God's Wonderful Railway would be complete without its locomotives, we will examine some of the technical changes and famous locos which moulded the engineering path of the company, and of the railway industry.

1

FORMATION

The Great Western Railway's roots lie in Bristol merchants' wish to maintain their city's status as the second great port of the country. Due to the increase in ship size and the gradual silting up of the River Avon, Liverpool was increasingly drawing a part of what had previously been Bristol's traffic. This was reinforced by the rail connection between Liverpool and London making transport easier.

In response, the Great Western Railway Company was incorporated by Act of Parliament on 31 August 1835, with powers to construct a railway between Bristol, Bath, Reading and London. Funds would be raised through £2.5 million in shares and £833,333 in loans, to a sum total of £3.33 million. This in itself was something of the GWR's most impressive achievement – getting off the ground. It was an awe-inspiring amount for the 1800s.

Isambard Kingdom Brunel was appointed as the engineer for the project. On his recommendation, the original proposal for the line of 4 ft 8½ inch gauge was scrapped in favour of the broad gauge 7 ft 0¼ inch, to allow for larger wheels outside the bodies of rolling stock that would give a smoother ride at higher speeds. This would later have the knock-on effect of the 'gauge

wars' with the LSWR, which made an impact on the company and on the whole industry.

The young engineer's second contraversial decision was the selection of the route for what would become the Great Western Main Line. This route, north of the Marlborough Downs, had no significant towns along its length, although it did offer potential links to Oxford and Gloucester.

Construction began in 1836, and the first 22.5 miles of the line, from Paddington to Maidenhead Bridge station, opened in 1838. The inaugural service was run by the 2-2-2 locomotive *North Star*, the GWR's first successful locomotive, running the 22 mile, 43 chain journey in 49 minutes. Regular services began on 4 June 1838.

The line crept west to Twyford by July 1839, and it was completed in sections thereafter, reaching Bristol Temple Meads in 1841.

This summary of the years between incorporation and completion of the initial line belies the many difficulties faced by Brunel and his associates in its construction. While construction of the line at the London end was relatively simple, with the

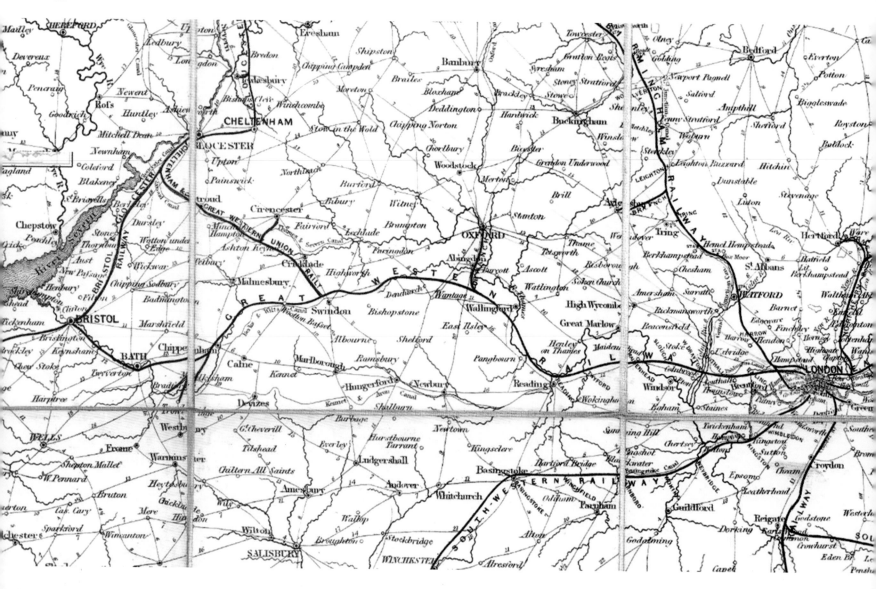

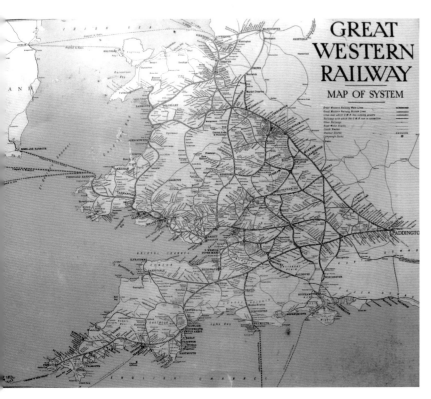

Left: Cheffin's 1850 map of the route of the GWR.

Above: A map of the system from around 1930, illustrating the incredible growth of the company's reach.

Right: Isambard Kingdom Brunel, the chief architect of the GWR, by the launching chains of the SS *Great Eastern*, 1857.

primary features causing any notable difficulty being the Sonning Cutting and the Maidenhead Railway Bridge, at the Bristol end it was another story entirely. Four bridges crossing the River Avon had to be constructed, as well as the Box Tunnel and eight other tunnels. The Box Tunnel itself was the final barrier to the realisation of the main line, and services from Temple Meads to Paddington began on completion in June 1841.

The company went from strength to strength, and despite a numbers of setbacks would eventually become one of the principal railway companies in the United Kingdom. Though the original route, or Great Western Main Line, ran between Bristol and London, the company soon expanded, extending into the Midlands, reaching Birmingham through Oxford in 1852 and Wolverhampton in 1854. The Shrewsbury & Birmingham Railway and the Shrewsbury & Chester Railway both amalgamated with the GWR at this time.

A number of issues were thrown up by Brunel's original decision to use a 7ft broad gauge for his railways. Comparatively, the London & South Western Railway was built on standard gauge (4 ft 8½ in) and thus any newly proposed route was bitterly contested as to which gauge would be used, as this would determine which company and its allies would hold commercial precedence in any particular area. The rivalry between the standard and broad gauge companies became known as the 'gauge wars'.

The gauge wars, however, were eventually lost, and mixed gauge became a common feature along the GWR's routes over the following years. The South Wales Railway amalgamated with the GWR in 1862 along with the West Midland Railway and the Oxford, Worcester & Wolverhampton Railway. The Bristol & Exeter Railway followed in 1876, followed by the South Devon Railway and, later, the Cornwall Railway in 1889.

The company continued to expand and standardise the gauge of the railways within its territories over the coming years, up until the First World War and amalgamation of the railways into the 'Big Four'. By 1930, the GWR had spread across much of Southern England, as seen on the previous page, becoming something of the giant of industry that we remember today. Not only did the company cover the major railway routes of the South, but also air, coach and water services across the country.

On top of these transport industries, it was also responsible in large part for the development of the tourist industry in the South of England, through its impressive advertising campaigns. Posters, books, films and other media were exploited to the full, far ahead of its competitors of the time. Specific campaigns made a large impact on the public subconscious, including the Cornish Riviera advertising, and hundreds of publications still exist which were either sponsored or produced by the company in order to promote its line and the destinations along its route.

Further, through the works of engineers and architects such as Isambard Kingdom Brunel, a lasting impact upon the architecture and landscape of the country was made, with 'impossible' bridges and tunnels, now listed buildings, created to make the railway's path possible, and many other celebrated constructs such as station buildings built.

Last, and by no means least, the formation of the GWR led in truth to a century of incredible developments and revolutionary designs in transport technology, with records for speed broken and achievements of mileage covered lauded. The GWR's engineers and in particular the Swindon railway works were central to the locomotive building industry, and produced many incredible achievements over the years.

Waverley Class 4-4-0 *Antiquary*, based at Swindon. It was built in 1855 and withdrawn in 1876.

In 1833, Isambard Kingdom Brunel was appointed chief engineer of the Great Western Railway, running from London to Bristol and later Exeter. The company was founded at a meeting in Bristol in 1833, and incorporated by Act of Parliament in 1835. It was Brunel's vision that passengers would be able to buy one ticket at London Paddington and travel all the way from London to New York, changing from the Great Western Railway to the *Great Western* steamship in Neyland.

Sir Daniel Gooch was was an English railway and transatlantic cable engineer, recruited by Isambard Kingdom Brunel for the Great Western Railway, under the title 'Superintendent of Locomotive Engines', taking office on 18 August 1837. In 1840, Gooch identified the site of Swindon Works, and in 1846 designed the first locomotive to be constructed there, *Great Western*, a prototype of the GWR Iron Duke Class.

2-2-2 *North Star*, the first successful locomotive owned by the GWR.

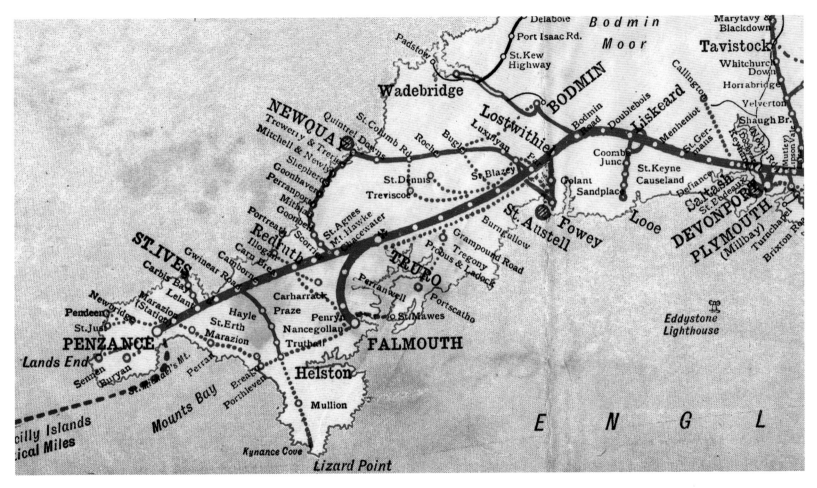

A map of the GWR in Cornwall.

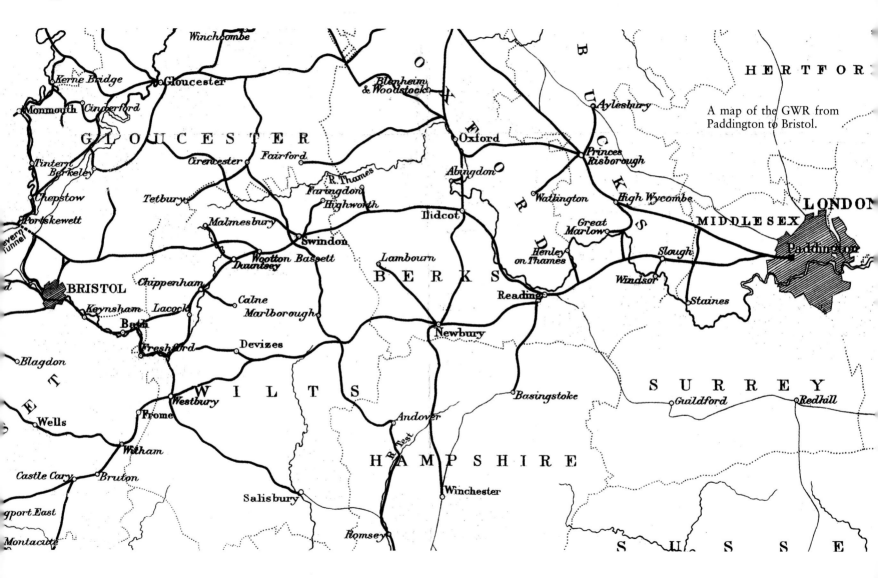

A map of the GWR from Paddington to Bristol.

2

ADVERTISING

One of the major industries in which the GWR was involved, and which is sometimes underestimated, was as one of the first publicity powerhouses of the 1900s. It exploited almost every available media, new and old, in order to further its exposure across the country and promote new lines, services and other products.

As early as 1903, it began to coin names for itself such as 'The Holiday Line'. In its own short firm, *The Story of a Holiday*, it advertised its services at the London Coliseum. It later began to publish books and gazetteers of holiday destinations and accommodation details, such as *Holiday Haunts*, which focused on resorts and locations along each of its lines. It also produced publications of specific locations, such as S. Mais' *The Cornish Riviera*, coining the term for one of its expresses.

As well as through film and literature, the company employed many artists in the production of its famous posters, several of which are included on the following pages. Not only did these advertise specific locations, and areas such as the aforementioned 'Cornish Riviera', but a plethora of other nuances and side projects, including publicity for the speed of GWR services, postal services, camping holidays in rail coaches, passenger services for canines, air services, bus services and specific events, such as horse racing. These posters could be found at any station and at the turn of the century was a media campaign rivalled only by governmental propoganda.

This comprehensive campaign, while primarily raising the company's profile and advertising the GWR and its services, also did much for the tourism industry, exploiting as it did some of the major media of the time.

Great Western Railway

2 HOURS
SHORTEST ROUTE

"Splendid run!
Thank You!"

LONDON
(Paddington) and
BIRMINGHAM
(Snow Hill)

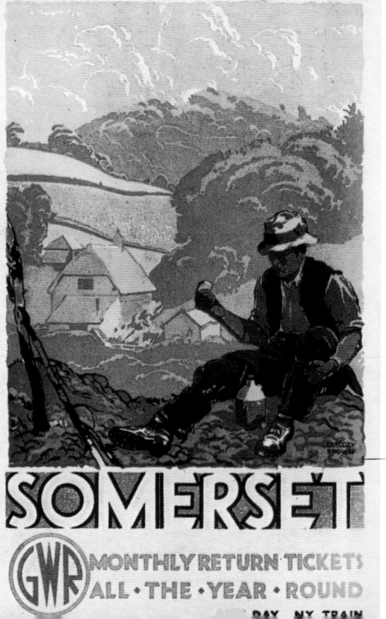

SOMERSET

GWR MONTHLY RETURN TICKETS
ALL·THE·YEAR·ROUND

Far left: Advertising the Paddington to Birmingham Express, only two hours.

Left: The Bristol & Exeter Railway amalgamated with the GWR in 1876, providing further reach for the company into Somerset, Devon, and later through to Cornwall.

Right: A fine example of one of the many posters promoting the direct travel to the capital.

RONALD LAMPITT

DEVON

This spread The GWR promoted the Devon and Cornwall coasts as the ideal holiday destination, including some beautiful artwork on some of their posters and adverts. Major tourist destinations included Minehead, Dartmouth and Torquay in Devon and Somerset, with the Cornish Riviera Express taking passengers through Taunton, Exeter, Plymouth, St Austell, Truro, Redruth and through to Penzance.

CORNWALL

MONTHLY RETURN TICKETS **GWR** **ANY DAY ANY TRAIN ANYWHERE**

Left: GWR poster for Oxford.

Right: A GWR poster for Ross-on-Wye.

SEND IT IN ADVANCE

BY

G.W.R

COLLECTED
CONVEYED
AND
DELIVERED

2/-
PER PACKAGE

CAMP-COACH
HOLIDAYS

NOVEL
AND ECONOMICAL
CAMPING
IN COMFORT

GWR

IN SELECTED
BEAUTY SPOTS OF SOMERSET
DEVON, CORNWALL AND WALES

Far left: An advert for the GWR's 'send it by advance' service, allowing passengers to travel luggage free and meet their belongings at their final destination.

Left: Camping coaches were offered by many railway companies in the United Kingdom as accommodation for holiday makers in rural or coastal areas. The coaches were old passenger vehicles no longer suitable for use in trains, which were converted to provide basic sleeping and living space at static locations. Many of the coaches would be removed from their stations in the winter and overhauled at the railway's workshops ready to be returned in the spring, being placed on sidings. The local railway staff looked after the coaches as part of their duties.

Right: An advert for passengers of the canine persuasion.

William Powell Frith's incredible canvas, *The Railway Station*. The *Times* stated, regarding the painting, 'the subject and the price of Mr Frith's picture alike belong to the time. The one is typical of our age of iron and steam; the other is only possible in a period of bold speculation, enterprising publishers and picture-dealers, a large print-buying and picture-seeing public, and great facilities for bringing that public and their shillings to a focus.'

G·W·R·
THE HOLIDAY LINE

HOLIDAY HAUNTS

1912 Edition

Price
3d.

Now Ready

THOUSANDS OF ADDRESSES OF
HOLIDAY ACCOMMODATION

"Best of its kind"
VIDE PRESS.

OBTAIN YOUR HOLIDAY ACCOMMODATION IN ADVANCE
Copies on Sale at all Bookstalls Stations and
Offices Price 3d. or Post Free 6d. Stamps from
Mr C. ALDINGTON, Superintendent of the Line PADDINGTON STATION W.

BIRMINGHAM
AIRPORT

CARDIFF
AIRPORT

HALDON
AERODROME — TEIGNMOUTH
PLYMOUTH   TORQUAY
AIRPORT

GWR
AIR SERVICES
BIRMINGHAM
CARDIFF
TEIGNMOUTH
TORQUAY
PLYMOUTH

Far left: The GWR collaborated in many publications to help further promote travel and tourism. This advert details *Holiday Haunts*, a gazetteer of holiday accommodation and advice. *Holiday Haunts* was the official GWR holiday guide, published annually in March.

Left: The GWR inaugurated the first railway air service between Cardiff, Torquay and Plymouth in association with Imperial Airways. This grew to become part of the Railway Air Services. The RAS was formed in 1934 by the 'Big Four' and Imperial Airways. It was a domestic airline serving the United Kingdom and a few associated territories.

Right: Another poster, this time advertising the charms of the coastal resort of Weston-super-Mare, near Bristol.

WESTON
SUPER - MARE
GWR *in Smiling Somerset* LMS
Guide FREE from A.R.Turner, Town Hall, Weston Super-Mare

Left: The Great Western Railway operated all the trains to Newquay from 1 October 1877 and bought out the Cornwall Minerals Railway on 1 July 1896. It later created the Truro & Newquay Railway, completed in 1905 and closed in 1963.

Right: Bath station was built in 1840 for the GWR, designed by Isambard Kingdom Brunel. Here we see the city advertised in all its architectural glory.

BATH

G·W·R

Great Western Railway

RACES

AT CARDIFF,
APRIL 22nd AND 23rd.

ON EACH OF THE ABOVE DATES,

CHEAP RETURN TICKETS

WILL BE ISSUED TO

CARDIFF

AS UNDER

At about a Single Fare and a quarter for the Double Journey.

FROM		Times of Starting.		Times of Return.	
		am		pm	
Cheltenham	-	8	45	6	10
Gloucester	-	9	17	6	10
Grange Court	-	9	31	4	5
Newnham	-	9	39		
Lydney	-	9	52	6	10
Chepstow	-	10	9		

Children under Three years of age, Free; Three, and under Twelve. Half price

The Tickets are not Transferable, and are available only by the Trains specified and between the Stations named upon them; if used otherwise, the full Ordinary Fare will be charged

NO LUGGAGE ALLOWED.

[H.D 43.] Paddington. April. 1890

HY. LAMBERT, General Manager.

2985a

Great Western Railway

SOUTH WALES
for Bracing Holidays

TENBY
SWANSEA
the MUMBLES
BARRY
BARRY ISLAND
PORTHCAWL
GOWERLAND
SAUNDERSFOOT

Atlantic Breezes
and Golden Sands

Far left: A GWR poster advertising the Cardiff Races, 1890.

Left: The GWR has had many nicknames, such as 'God's Wonderful Railway' and the 'Great Way Round', but it was famed as the 'Holiday Line', taking passengers from across the country to the holiday resorts of the south-west and southern Wales.

Right: A poster advertising some of the GWR's long-distance services from London to the West and Midlands, giving the exact distances and times of each journey. The speed of the GWR's expresses was one of their major publicity angles, with a record 66.2 mph booked on a Swindon to Paddington express in 1929.

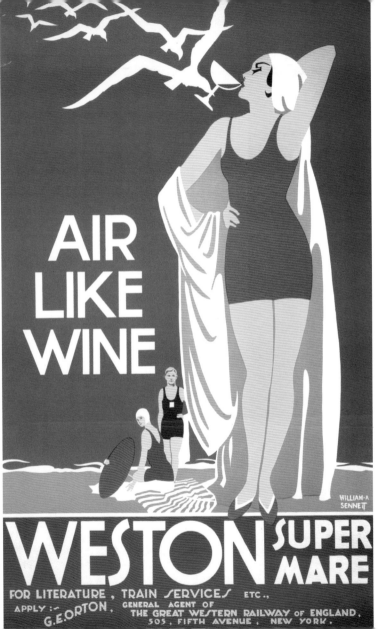

Left: This poster advertises the apparent similarities in climate between Italy and Cornwall. Some artistic license may have been taken with the maps' dimensions.

Right: Another advert for the popular holiday destination of Weston-super-Mare.

Left: Powers were granted by Parliament for the GWR to operate ships in 1871. The company thereafter operated ships on the route between Neyland, Wales, and Waterford, Ireland.

Right: Further expanding the company's reach, the GWR operated motor services in several areas not served by rail. These ran from 1903 to 1933 in areas that were otherwise not served by rail.

CLIFTON SUSPENSION BRIDGE

BRISTOL

GWR Illustrated Booklets from Development Board, BRISTOL LMS

Left: One of the most well-known GWR posters, promoting the company's fast services to the West of England. This one pictures a King class locomotive. This image was created by Charles Mayo in 1939.

Right: A poster advertising one of the illustrated booklets provided by the GWR. The company were involved in many such publications on specific holiday destinations, akin to the first travel agency guides. By promoting the locations they also promoted their own services, massively enhancing the British tourist industry during the nineteenth and twentieth centuries.

Left: An advert for the route to Ireland via Fishguard. The Welsh terminus of the GWR was relocated to Fishguard when the railway reached there in 1906.

Right: Passengers were drawn to the idea of travelling to Cornwall on the GWR, after the company advertised S. Mais' book *The Cornish Riviera*. The term was thereafter used widely in their adverts.

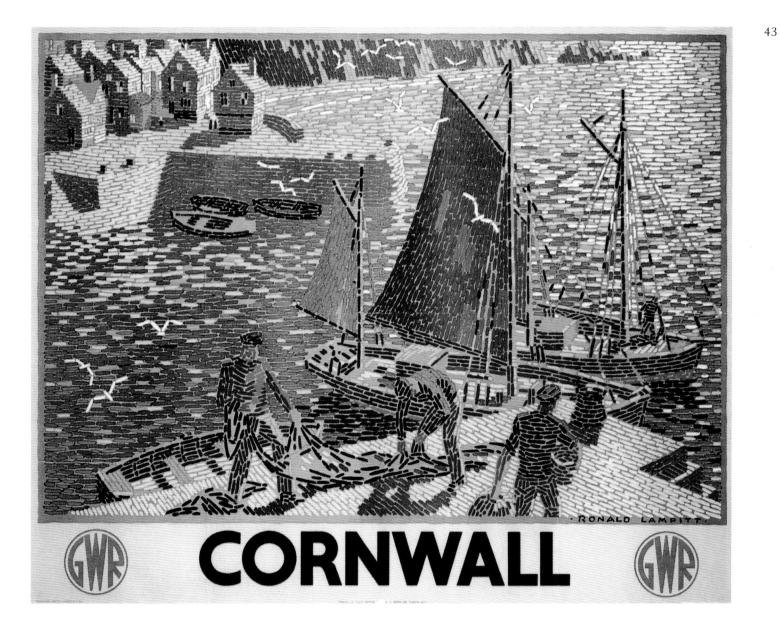

CORNWALL

This spread: More examples of the GWR's 'Cornish Riviera' advertising.

THE "KING" OF RAILWAY LOCOMOTIVES

16000

A Great Western Railway Book of Britain's Mightiest Passenger Locomotive

TRACK TOPICS

FULLY ILLUSTRATED · ONE SHILLING

A BOOK OF RAILWAY ENGINEERING FOR BOYS OF ALL AGES

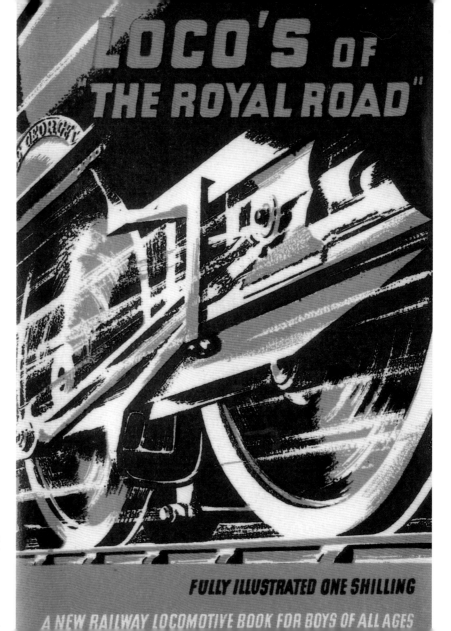

This spread: A number of examples of the books published by the GWR for 'boys of all ages', and perhaps the origin of an industry of which this publication is a part.

BRUNEL and After

The Romance of the **GREAT WESTERN RAILWAY**

PRICE ONE SHILLING

"CAERPHILLY CASTLE"

A GREAT WESTERN RAILWAY BOOK

This spread: Several other examples of the GWR's foray into the publishing industry, including titles focused on the company's legendary engineer and a focus on the engines themselves.

A map of the stations and route of the GWR's 'Cornish Riviera', 'England's national health and pleasure resort'.

3

ARCHITECTURE

Continuing our lateral view of the GWR as an industry, the sheer scope and size of the company, stretching as it did across a large portion of mainland England and Wales and surviving for over 100 years, ensured that it had a lasting impact upon the country's architecture.

There are no fewer than fifty Grade I and II listed stations, associated railway buildings, bridges and structures which were designed, built or modified by the GWR and its engineers and architects during its lifetime, and six major museums which are either located in GWR buildings or dedicated to the GWR itself. These include Bristol Temple Meads railway station, Avon Bridge in Bristol, Swindon Works (which in itself had a singularly massive effect on the prosperity and growth of the town over the last century), the Box Tunnel, Wiltshire and Maidenhead Railway Bridge.

Due partly to this, and to the historical significance these buildings and constructs pose, UNESCO is even considering a proposal to list the Great Western Main Line as a World Heritage Site. This would focus on several individual sites, including Bristol Temple Meads, Bath Spa station, the Swindon area, Maidenhead Railway Bridge, Wharncliffe Viaduct and London Paddington.

It could be argued that the GWR and its engineers and architect changed the face of the country and its landscape forever.

Temple Meads Station. 840.

The original terminus of Bristol Temple Meads was built between 1839 and 1841 for the GWR by Isambard Kingdom Brunel. The station was on a viaduct to raise it over the Floating Harbour and the River Avon. It was covered by a 200-foot train shed, covering the platforms, storage area and engine shed, and with a Tudor style frontage containing offices. Train services commenced on 31 August 1840. To the left can be seen the main entrance of the station as built in 1870, while to the right is the entrance to Brunel's original station.

Locomotives under steam at
Bristol Temple Meads.

An old engraving of the interior of the station.

An early illustration of Brunel's original station at Temple Meads.

Brunel's Avon Bridge in Bristol as it looked in 1846. Built in 1839 to carry the Great Western Main Line into Temple Meads station, it is now a Grade I listed building.

This spread: Bath Spa was designed and built by Brunel in 1840 for the GWR. Its Tudor style building with curving gables in an excellent example of Brunel's work. The station was opened on 31 August 1840. It was originally named simply 'Bath', but later they added the 'Spa' element to distinguish from Bath Green Park station in 1949.

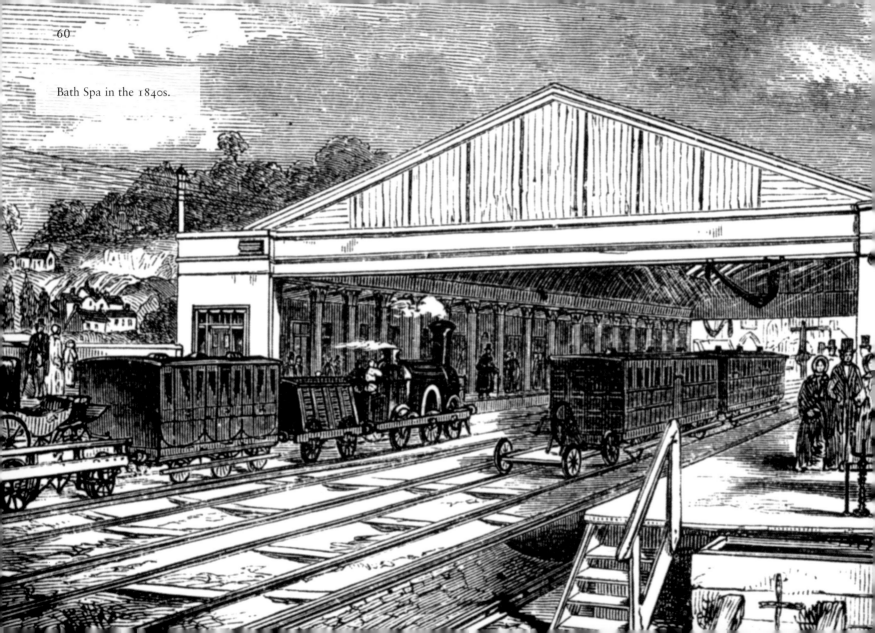

Bath Spa in the 1840s.

There are several good myths about how the GWR's route ended up passing through Swindon. One of these states that Brunel and Daniel Gooch threw a stone, or dropped a sandwich, on the spot while viewing a location nearby, and declared the spot perfect for the works. It seems more likely that the geography of Swindon in the middle of several GWR stations was the true reason. Nonetheless, Gooch identified the site in 1840 and in 1841 the directors of the company authorised establishment of the works at Swindon. It became operational in 1843, with the station opening in 1842 for services. This image shows Swindon around 1850.

Swindon station, 1950.

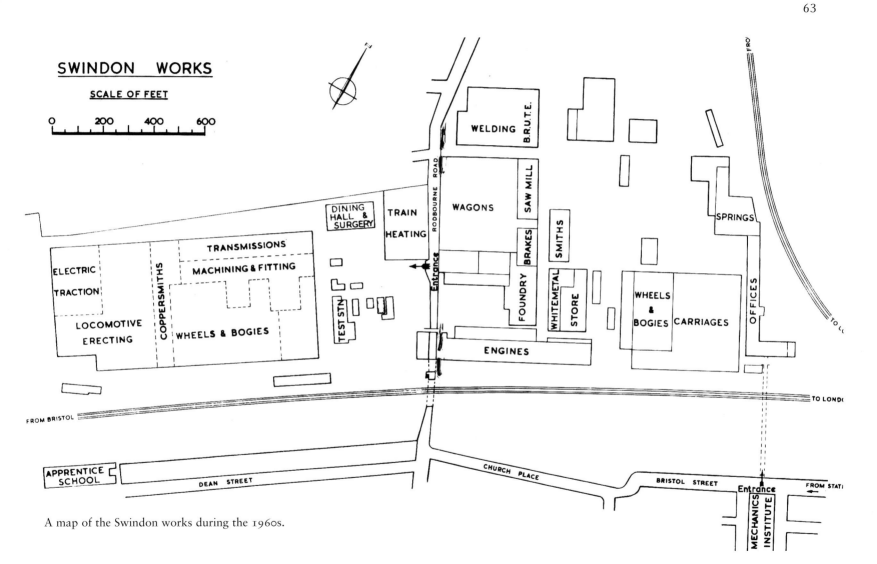

A map of the Swindon works during the 1960s.

The works initially employed around 200 men, and were responsible for repairs initially. The first locomotive, *Premier*, was built in 1846, later renamed *Great Western*. By 1851 the works had expanded massively, with over 2,000 employees. The works continued to expand, reaching around 14,000 people employed in the 1940s. Swindon owes a lot of its expansion to the works, changing it from a small village of 2,500 people to the town it is today. Sadly, with the onset of diesel and nationalisation, the works declined post-Second World War and eventually closed. Today, the works has been redeveloped and is now the Swindon Steam Railway Museum, hosting many fine examples of the GWR's heritage as seen opposite.

The original Reading station (*above*) was opened in 1840 as a temporary terminus at the western extent of the GWR. The line was later extended to Bristol with completion of that section of the line. As seen on this spread, it was a standard Brunellian station design, single-sided with seperate Up and Down platforms. In 1860, a new station building was constructed (*opposite*) for the GWR. Since then the station has been through several incarnations. Today it is the third busiest interchange station outside of London, with around 3.8 million passengers annually.

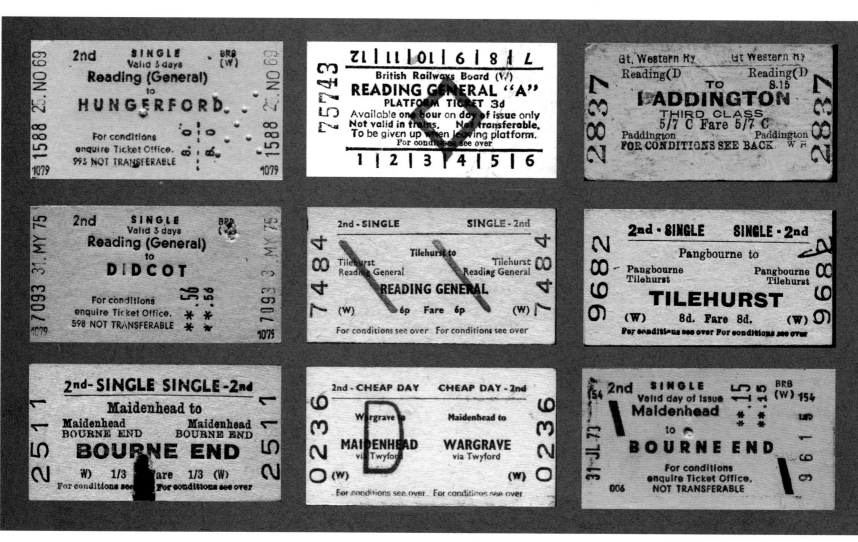

Some examples of tickets for Reading and Maidenhead.

This image shows the first station at Maidenhead, built in 1838. The present station at Maidenhead is effectively the fourth to bear that name.

Maidenhead railway bridge, also known as the Viaduct or Sounding Arch, was designed by Brunel and completed in 1838. At the time of building, these arches were the 'flattest' in the world. It is believed that the GWR didn't think that the arches would hold up under the weight of the locomotives passing. Evidence seems to suggest that these critics were incorrect.

A more recent view of Maidenhead station.

The third Maidenhead station, replaced by its current incarnation.

Paddington station was first opened as a temporary terminus for the GWR in 1838. The main station opened in 1854, and the original temporary building became the goods depot. The station was designed by Brunel, and a sketch of the interior can be seen above.

These two images, taken from the *Illustrated London News*, show the temporary station of 1838.

This image shows Platform 1 around 1950. The main station building was designed by Brunel, although much of the architectural detail was completed by Matthew Digby Wyatt. The station has been rebuilt and extended on multiple occasions since it was originally built, most notably during the 1890s and 1900s. Today, Paddington sports fourteen terminal plantforms. Platforms 1–8 are below the original spans of Brunel's train shed.

One of the side entrances to Paddington. Due to the positioning of the Great Western Hotel, passengers had to enter and exit via two side entrances. This image shows the entrance on the arrival side.

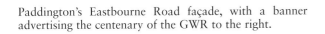

Paddington's Eastbourne Road façade, with a banner advertising the centenary of the GWR to the right.

This area, known as 'The Lawn', was originally occupied by a series of turntables and transverse sidings, designed to manually transfer locos between lines.

Paddington today.

No. 50044 *Exeter* platformed beneath Brunel's
wrought-iron roof.

Wharncliffe Viaduct was the first major structural design by Isambard Kingdom Brunel, the first contract to be let on the GWR and the first major engineering work completed. At 886 feet long, with eight arches, the supporting piers are hollow and tapered, rising to projecting stone cornices. It was one of the very first structures to be listed as Grade I, 1949, and is one of the key areas covered by the bid to make the GWR main line a World Heritage site.

Proposed in the 1835
Great Western Railway
Act, the Box Tunnel
between Bath and
Chippenham was at
the time considered
an impossible feat of
engineering. At 1.83
miles long, descending
on a 1 in 100 gradient,
construction began
in 1838, overseen by
Brunel, and the tunnel
opened to traffic in
1841. It is one of
the most significant
structures on the Great
Western Main Line.

4

LOCOMOTIVES

Naturally, this wouldn't be a complete book about the Great Western Railway if one did not consider the locomotives themselves.

GWR locomotives' designs were originally specified by Isambard Kingdom Brunel, although Daniel Gooch was later appointed as the Locomotive Superintendent of the railway. He went on to design several main broad gauge locos for the railway. Gooch was later succeeded by Joseph Armstrong who took loco design in his own direction, relying in part on his standard gauge experience. On his death, Armstrong was succeeded by William Dean, who developed the 4-4-0 type. The flagship 4-6-0s were initially introduced by engineer Charles Churchward. Collett took over in 1921, standardising the many types of engine in service by that time, and introducing the iconic Castle and King classes. Frederick Hawksworth then took charge in 1941, producing GWR locos until after nationalisation in 1941.

Throughout the GWR's history, and especially after the Railways Act of 1921 brought most independent companies in the area under GWR control, the number of locos controlled by the company was massive. Swindon Works was still producing over sixty locos per year even after Nationalisation, so one can imagine what numbers looked like during its peak years. Here we'll take a look at some examples of the GWR's engineering portfolio, and how the company used its powers to further transport technology throughout the last century.

GWR 4-2-2 Iron Duke class No. 3046 *Lord of the Isles*, built in 1851. This locomotive enjoyed a deal of attention after being chosen as the prototype for a Tri-ang model locomotive.

A GWR London to
Birmingham express,
hauled by a Duke Class
4-4-0.

No. 102 *La France* was purchased by Churchward in order to view French locomotives in practice. It is visibly not a GWR-built locomotive, with differences to firebox and cab. *La France* worked expresses including the inaugural Down Cornish Riviera express in 1904. Compared with GWR locos, it was found to produce a much smoother ride and a reduction in the loads on the rods and axleboxes. *La France* was withdrawn in 1926 after running over 700,000 miles. It had a lasting effect on many locomotive designers, including Churchward, Stanier and Riddles.

GWR 2-6-0 No. 33, which appeared in 1900.

GWR 4-6-0 No. 6014 *King Henry VII* with the Up Bristolian.

The broad gauge 4-2-2 *Great Western*. Rebuilt from the 2-2-2, the GWR's first prototype loco. This was one of the pioneers of the GWR's loco building industry, built in 1846 and withdrawn in 1870.

4-2-2 No. 3069 *Earl of Chester* passes Hayes on an Up
Birmingham express around 1908.

4-4-0 No. 3701 *Stanley Baldwin* leaving Paddington around 1910.

No. 171 *Albion* on the Cornish Riviera express, shown on a Christmas postcard.

4-4-2 No. 104 *Alliance.*

4-6-0 No. 4013 *Knight of St Patrick* during the First World War.

4-6-2 No. 111 *The Great Bear* on the Cornish Riviera express. *The Great Bear* was the first 4-6-2, built in 1908 and considered the GWR's flagship locomotive until 1923. At the time, this was one of the largest locomotives in the UK. In practice, although larger in size, it did not improve massively on existing classes performance, and its 20 ton 9 cwt axle load limited it to the Paddington to Bristol main line. Thus, this image of the train on the Cornish Riviera express expresses some artistic license. The GWR did not opt for the Pacific wheel arrangement in the end, sticking with the 4-6-0 arrangement as their stalwart. Thus, in 1924, *The Great Bear* was rebuilt as a 4-6-0 Castle class and renamed *Viscount Churchill*, retaining the No. 111. It was later withdrawn from service in 1953.

The Great Bear was the first 4-6-2 to be built in the UK and the only 4-6-2 designed by George Churchward. Here it is seen departing Paddington's Platform 1.

Castle class 4-6-0 No. 4079 *Pendennis Castle*, preserved at Didcot Railway Centre. No. 4079 was built at Swindon Works in 1924. It became famous in 1925 when lent to the LNER for trials against the A1 Pacific class. The loco made the journey from King's Cross to Finsbury Park in times of less than six minutes, beating the Pacific class. It was also more economical in its use of fuel. *Pendennis Castle* was removed from service in 1964. In 2005, it was restored and installed at Didcot Railway Centre.

King class 4-6-0 No. 6023 *King Edward II* on display at the Didcot Railway Centre in 2013. Built at Swindon Works in 1930, it worked the expresses between London and Devon for much of its life. It was withdrawn from service in 1962. Although originally sentenced for breaking up, it passed through several hands before being restored at Didcot by the Great Western Society. In 2011 it re-entered service, making several appearances on the Great Central Railway.

King class No. 6024 *King Edward I*, which ran from 1930 to 1962. The locomotive is currently undergoing a heavy overhaul at the West Somerset Railway workshops in Minehead.

57XX class 0-6-0PT No. 3738, built at Swindon in 1937.

Hall class 4-6-0 No. 4965 *Rood Ashton Hall* and No. 4953 *Earl of Mount Edgcumbe* under steam in 2011.

King class 4-6-0 No. 6024 *King Edward I* in 2006.

Castle class 4-6-0 No.
5029 *Nunney Castle* and
No. 6024 *King Edward I*
en route from Penzance to
Bristol.

A *North Star* replica,
built to celebrate the
GWR's centenary, now
housed at the Swindon
Steam Railway
Museum.

Hall class 4-6-0 No. 4931 *Hanbury Hall*, built in 1929 and withdrawn from service in 1962.

Castle class 4-6-0 No. 5029 *Nunney Castle* was built at Swindon Works in 1934. The loco was used in a number of publicity materials on the GWR over the years. *Nunney Castle* was sold in 1964 and sat in a scrap yard for over ten years. The loco was sold and returned to the main line in the 1990s. After a major overhaul, it has now been in use since 2008.

Class 4MT 2-6-4T Nos 80080 and 80079
approaching Tiverton Parkway.

Class 4MT 2-6-4T Nos 80079 and 80080 again.

Achilles class 4-2-2 leaving Exeter St Davids with the Flying Dutchman service.

The GWR built a prototype 2-6-2T loco in 1904 with 4 ft 1 inch coupled wheels. Ten further engines of this type were produced, becoming the 31XX class. This later became the 44XX class, operating on the Kingsbridge branch. This image shows No. 3104.

45XX No. 2185 at Brent around 1910. This loco was built in 1909 and later became No. 4535 in 1912.

A Duke class 4-4-0 at Bitteford. This class had outside frames and parallel domed boilers. Designed by WIlliam Dean, they were built in five batches between 1895 and 1899 for express services.

A Collett 14XX class 0-4-2T No. 1463, built at Swindon in 1936 and withdrawn in 1961. It is seen here at Didcot.

City class 4-4-0 No. 3440 *City of Truro* was designed by George Churchward and built at Swindon in 1903. It wrote a place in history as one of the possible contenders for the first steam loco to reach in excess of 100 mph, although the factual accuracy of the measurement which led to this claim has been much disputed over the years. The loco has been rebuilt and restored several times, and recently withdrawn from service due to the extent of repairs needed to keep it running.

5

OTHER SERVICES

The ambitions of the GWR were not merely confined to the railway, belying its name. The Great Western Railway road motor services operated from 1903 to 1933, the first successful bus services operated by a British railway company. Rather than paying the estimated £85,000 to build a light railway to serve the area south of Helston in Cornwall, they decided to test market bus services, acquiring two vehicles used by the Lynton & Barnstaple Railway. Proving to be a popular addition, further routes were soon established. By 1904, thirty-six services were in operation, with several in London. The first vehicles used with 16hp Milnes-Daimler single-deck buses, followed by 20hp and 30hp versions. The main areas services ran in were Devon, Cornwall and Slough.

As well as road transport, the GWR also led a foray into air services, helping to form Railway Air Services with the three other railway companies in the 'Big Four' and Imperial Airways. The airline operated domestic routes within the United Kingdom.

Finally, the GWR also owned a bumber of ships which operated in conjunction with their railways to provide services over to Ireland, the Channel Islands and France. An Act of Parliament granted powers to operate ships in 1871. Isambard Kingdom Brunel envisaged a route the stretched from London in the east to the USA in the west, all on the GWR. This dream was never quite realised, as transatlantic travel from Bristol became unlikely as services moved to the more accommodating port of Liverpool, but the GWR operated a number of services and ships during its tenure.

An Imperial Airways Westland Wessex hired by the GWR in 1933 to work its air services. See the GWR crest on its tail.

GWR 20hp Milnes-Daimler AF 64 fleet No. 5, outside the Royal Hart Hotel, Beaconsfield, terminus of the route from Slough.

The SS *Great Western* at Weymouth on the Channel Islands service. The GWR had a tramway running through the streets to the quay on the far side of the vessel.

The Great Western Royal Hotel was designed by P. Hardwick and Brunel in the French Renaissance style. The building lost many of its ornamental balastrudes during the 1930s, and so appears today much different to this image from the turn of the century. Brunel was the hotel's first managing director, and funding came largely from the GWR. It cost approximately £60,000 to build. Brunel's idea was that a passenger the GWR's reach should extend from the point where a passenger entered the Great Western Royal Hotel until they reached New York. These grand ambitions never came to fruition as the *Great Western* was scrapped before completion of the hotel. However, the hotel survives today as the Hilton London Paddington.

A view of the Waterford Quay. The GWR commenced passenger services from Fishguard to Waterford, Ireland, in 1872. In the background can be seen several GWR ships docked. Although Brunel's transatlantic dreams may have fallen short, the company\s route was formidable, and its involvement in so many industries belies its name as the Great Western Railway.